HOPPY
THE
MAGPIE

Bronwyn A Filsell

Illustrated by Samantha Brandt

Hoppy the Magpie
Copyright © 2023 by Bronwyn A Filsell

All rights reserved. No part of this publication may be reproduced, distributed, or transmitted in any form or by any means, including photocopying, recording, or other electronic or mechanical methods, without the prior written permission of the author, except in the case of brief quotations embodied in critical reviews and certain other non-commercial uses permitted by copyright law.

Tellwell Talent
www.tellwell.ca

ISBN
978-0-2288-9573-2 (Paperback)

Look! Look! There's a baby magpie on the lawn. It's a girl magpie because she has black speckles in her white feathers. Isn't she pretty? Magpies eat worms and grubs. They like meat. It keeps them strong. Lots of bugs to eat too...yum.

Hoppy has something wrong with her leg. It won't work properly. She can only hop on one leg. She can't run like her Mum, Dad and sister. But she is still fast. Look at her hop along.

She tries so hard to keep up.

Mr and Mrs Magpie feed the other baby first. They push the food into the baby's beak.

Baby magpies make a lot of noise when they are hungry. Hoppy waits for her Mum to put the food in her beak. She is so, so hungry because she is growing.

Mother Magpie pushes in some mashed up insects which she caught.

Hoppy swallows them down and then calls for more.

Then they all fly to the gum trees and Mother magpie makes the baby birds wait in the tree for her while she finds more food.

They visit the lawn every day. There is a big dog living there who likes magpies and she has a friend who is a cat. The cat is nice to birds. The lady likes the grown up magpies to sit on the clothes line. She talks to them. They look down at her and listen.

The lady gives them food when there is no rain to make the ground soft to dig for worms.

This is a friendly place.

There are lots of water bowls around and a bird bath out the front. Magpies like to have a bath. They like to get clean and to cool down in very hot weather.

Hoppy is different from her family. She has one leg that works while they have two legs. She can't keep up with them now. Her parents notice this. They give her sister more food than Hoppy. She has to push in to get fed. Her sister yells at her. They fight over the food.

Something is changing. The lady too can see that Hoppy's family are pushing her away.

The lady is very worried. She tells Hoppy that she will help feed her. Hoppy does not understand. But the lady feeds her every day.

The lady puts some dog mince on top of the wood shed for the magpie family. It is summer and the earth is hard and dry. The magpies can't find enough food in the bush.

All the magpies are very hungry. In the bird world only the strong healthy birds get all the food. Sick birds miss out. There is no-one to help them get food.

The lady feeds the magpie family and watches. She hides behind the garden shed and peeks out.

Would Hoppy get some food or would her family eat it all?

"Well I never!" said the lady. "Hoppy's family are letting her eat with them now."

Hoppy has grown stronger and her family see this. She can run nearly as fast as they can because she tries SO hard. The dog mince is helping her leg to get strong too.

Hoppy is very cheeky. She runs to the lady's back door and calls out in magpie talk.

She is asking for food and the lady brings her cat biscuits.

The lady throws them onto the lawn and Hoppy runs to each little biscuit and picks it up in her long beak.

She eats them all and is very happy.

One day the lady was outside and Hoppy flew down from the house roof. Something looked strange about her. There was something not right. The lady looked closer. Oh no!

What could have happened? Where is Hoppy's top beak? There was only a tiny bit left.

Her beak had broken off.

How would Hoppy eat? The lady was very worried. She could see Hoppy's long silver tongue poking out. The lady got some dog mince and put it on the lawn.

Hoppy tried very hard to pick it up but she could not. Her top beak was very short and could not grab onto the bottom beak. But Hoppy was very clever. She tried another way to eat the mince. Hoppy tipped her head to the side and scooped the meat up in her long bottom beak.

One morning Hoppy's family were staring at her. Oh no, what could be wrong?

The lady's neighbour is calling out. "Look at Hoppy, she has lost her bottom beak now".

The lady went over to Hoppy. This is bad. How will poor Hoppy eat?

Her long silver tongue was sticking out all the time now. It had no beak to rest on.

Hoppy was still a baby and so many things had gone wrong for her.

She had never given up and always found a way to get through.

Do you think she will find another way to eat?

Hoppy is a very pretty magpie. She has really long legs and very shiny eyes. Hoppy is always hungry and she has learnt to sing songs in magpie music. Her family still fly with her and keep her safe. They feed her when they can. The lady hopes Hoppy's family will still keep her in their family and not send her away.

It is evening and time for the magpies to eat their dog mince. They are waiting in the tall gum trees behind the wood shed. Hoppy is sitting next to her family.

The lady puts the dog mince on the iron roof and calls the magpies down. They fly softly over her head and land.

Their claws make a tapping on the roof as they walk around. Hoppy flies onto the lawn and the lady throws her some mince. She watches Hoppy pick it up in her very short beak.

Hoppy uses her very long tongue to scoop up some of the food. She is eating. She will not starve.

How happy the lady is. She lets her neighbour know that Hoppy will be okay if they feed her.

Without the lady's help Hoppy could not eat. She needs a long beak to grab the bugs and worms with. Magpies listen to the noises under the ground. They tip their heads to one side and when they hear a beetle or a worm they dig in the ground with their beak and then pull it out. Hoppy can't do this with a broken beak.

Hoppy will live in the trees near the lady. She will feed her every morning and night so that Hoppy will grow into a beautiful strong magpie.

Where is Hoppy today?

Here she is! Hoppy is lying on a log with her wings spread out wide to catch the warm sun.

She looks like she is asleep. Hoppy is having a special sun-bath that birds do.

She lies flat so that her feathers get all the sun.

The sun kills all the nasty lice and mites which can make birds very sick.

What an amazing magpie Hoppy is.

www.ingramcontent.com/pod-product-compliance
Lightning Source LLC
LaVergne TN
LVHW072018060526
838200LV00060B/4700